Crash Corrigan's Ranch
and
The Crash Corrigan Show

Featuring the Scripts for
August 19, 1950
and
April 14, 1951

Compiled by
Jerry L. Schneider

Corriganville Press
www.CorriganvillePress.com

ISBN 978-1312187672

Published by
Corriganville Press
www.CorriganvillePress.com

CRASH CORRIGAN'S RANCH
(Program Title)

_____
(Advertiser)

_____
(Agency)

BOB OLSEN
(Writer)

SATURDAY - AUGUST 19, 1950
(Day and Date)

8:00-8:30PM
(Time)

TELEVISION PRODUCTION NOTES

CHARACTERS AND CAST	PROPS AND SET
CRASH CORRIGAN	PER SCRIPT
GEORGIA LEE	
BOB OATES	
MAX "ALIBI" TERHUNE	
BUDDY MCDOWELL	
RALPH WARD	
THE BROOME BOYS WITH BILLY WOLFE	

SOUND	TITLE CARDS
ALARM CLOCK	Per Script

STUART PHELPS
(Production Director)

_____
(Production Assistant)

RUSSELL FURSE AND DAN ECKLEY
(Agency Producer or Announcer)

STANDARD OPENING   (THEME MUSIC).

(SUPER TITLES)

C.U. OF CORRIGAN   CORRIGAN: Welcome to Corrigan's Ranch!

I'm Crash Corrigan, who says, there's no

time like right now to have fun!

CAST: YIPPEE

CORRIGAN: Folks, I don't know about you

but I like good music...western music. And

just to show you how we work together here

at Corrigan's Ranch here's some sweet

harmony from.....

BUDDY: ONE MAN BAND

CORRIGAN: Buddy McDowell! Stop that

racket!

BUDDY: (KEEPS RIGHT ON PLAYING)

BROOME BOYS: (SHOUT HIM DOWN)   SHUDDUP!

BUDDY: What's the matter?

CORRIGAN: We're TRYING to get the show

started.

BUDDY: Well, I heard you say, "sweet

harmony". I thought that was my cue.

LEE BROOME: Your cue is "Drop dead".

BUDDY: Oh, I can do anything you Broome

Boys can do.

CORRIGAN: Okay, but the Broome Boys are

gonna do it. Go ahead, Boys, while it's

quiet.

MUSIC: ("SONG OF THE BANDIT" BROOME BOYS)

(APPLAUSE)

e

BUDDY: ONE MAN BAND

CORRIGAN: (INTERRUPTING AGAIN) Buddy!

BUDDY: (STOPS PLAYING)

CORRIGAN: (SHAKING HIS FINGER) Uh, uh.

BUDDY: I'm cheaper than the Broome Boys.

CORRIGAN: No dice, Buddy.

BUDDY: (WALKS UP TO CRASH AS IF TO STARE
        HIM DOWN ONLY, OF COURSE, HE STARES
        INTO CRASH' CHEST)

CORRIGAN: Buddy, you're not sore, are ya?

BUDDY: Just because you're bigger'n I am's

no sign I'm littler'n you are. (HE MAKES

AN IMAGINARY LINE ON THE FLOOR) Step across

that, I dare ya!

CORRIGAN: (STEPS ACROSS)

BUDDY: (ANOTHER LINE) Step across that.

CORRIGAN: (DOES IT)

BUDDY: (MAKES ONE MORE LINE) I'd like to

see you step across THAT line.

CORRIGAN: Okay. (STEPS ACROSS) Here I am.

BUDDY: Now you're on MY side, ain'tcha?

GEORGIA LEE ENTERS

(BUDDY HURRYS OFF AS GEORGIA LEE ENTERS)

CORRIGAN: Well, doggone, here's my little

ole foreman, MISS GEORGIA LEE!

CAST: (CHEERS)

GEORGIA: Hi gang! Crash, what's the matter

around here tonight?

CORRIGAN: Why?

GEORGIA: Everybody's arguin'. And YOU!

CORRIGAN: Who? Me?

e

GEORGIA: You usually start it!

CORRIGAN: I start it? Why, I'm the dove of peace.

GEORGIA: Dove, huh? And I suppose I didn't hear you and Bob Oates out there awhile ago?

CORRIGAN: Oh, THAT.

GEORGIA: Yes, THAT. Crash, there's only one way to live a good life.

CORRIGAN: How do you mean?

GEORGIA: Let's work together, boys.

MUSIC: ("ON THE SUNNY SIDE OF THE STREET")

(APPLAUSE)

CUT TO:

CORRIGAN AND BOB OATES.

GEORGIA: Thanks, gang.

CORRIGAN: Bob, Georgia Lee heard us fighting before the show.

BOB OATES: She did?

CORRIGAN: She says we should walk on the Sunny Side.

BOB OATES: You know, Crash, she's right.

CORRIGAN: Yeah. That was a silly argument anyway.

BOB OATES: That's what I thought when you brought it up.

CORRIGAN: I brought it up?

BOB OATES: Yes, YOU brought it up.

CORRIGAN: Is THAT so?

(THEY STAND TOE TO TOE FOR A MOMENT)

BOB OATES: Yes, THAT'S so.

CORRIGAN: By the way, what were we arguin' about?

BOB OATES: About that tour you gave up last week.

CRASH CORRIGAN'S RANCH
8-19-50

CORRIGAN: Oh, yeah. I said I thought
             I'd better go after all.

BOB OATES: And I said, it must be nice
             to go galavantin' around the
             country and leave all the work
             to your....and I quote...
             "pals". Besides.....

CORRIGAN: Besides what?

BOB OATES: Well, you go away...then, first
             thing you know Georgie Lee
             goes...then Alibi...then Buddy,
             Ralph Ward, the Broome Boys.
             See what you got left?

CORRIGAN: What?

MUSIC: "EMPTY SADDLES" BOB OATES

x

CRASH CORRIGAN'S RANCH
8-19-50

CORRIGAN: Hey, Bob, I've got an idea.

BOB OATES: Okay, what is it?

CORRIGAN: Let's you and me trade jobs.

BOB OATES: Good idea! Do we trade pay checks too?

CORRIGAN: Now here's how it works: you do the work I was doing up at the lake.

BOB OATES: Yeah.

CORRIGAN: And I'll work here at the barn.

BOB OATES: I'd better stick pretty close to the show, Crash.

CORRIGAN: I'll call you when we need you.

BOB OATES: That's fine, but what are you gonna do?

CORRIGAN: The horses need grooming.

BOB OATES: Okay, you work in the barn and I'll work at the lake.

(CRASH STARTS STRAIGHTENING HIS HAIR)

CORRIGAN: Do I look all right?

BOB OATES: What do you care, you're gonna work in the barn.

CORRIGAN: Yeah, well, I'll see ya.

BOB STARTS TO EXIT AS GEORGIA LEE ENTERS. BOB JOINS GEORGIA. CRASH RUSHES BACK AND JOINS GEORGIA ALSO.

GEORGIA: Hi, Bob.

BOB OATES: Hi, Georgie.

CORRIGAN: The lake, Bob. Remember?

BOB OATES: The barn, Crash. Remember?

GEORGIA: What's goin" on here, anyway?

BOB OATES: Isn't it time we sing our duet?

x

CORRIGAN: Oh, no. We're tradin' jobs. I sing the duet with Miss Georgia.

	BOB OATES:	Oh, yeah.
	CORRIGAN:	Yeah.
	BOB OATES:	I don't think so.
	CORRIGAN:	I think so.
	BOB OATES:	Oh, yeah.
THEY LEAN AGAINST EACH OTHER AND ACROSS GEORGIA LEE UNTIL SHE HAS TO DO A SQUAT TO KEEP FROM BEING CRUSHED. SHE WALKS OUT AND OVER TO RALPH WARD.	CORRIAN:	Yeah.
	GEORGIA:	Ralph.
	RALPH:	Hi, Georgie.
	GEORGIA:	Would you like to do a duet with me ?
CATCH A TAKE FROM BOB AND CORRIGAN JUST BEFORE THE NUMBER	RALPH:	Oh, YEAH!
	MUSIC:	"I'M ALABAMY BOUND" RALPH AND GEORGIA
CUT TO:	(APPLAUSE)	

X

ALIBI AND ELMER.	ALIBI:	So you're pretty sweet on Georgia Lee, huh?
	ELMER:	Let's put it this way, out of all the women I know.
	ALIBI:	Yes?
	ELMER:	I tolerate her the most often.
	ALIBI:	And when don't you tolerate her?
	ELMER:	When she sings duets with that Ralph Ward.
	ALIBI:	And how does she feel about you?
	ELMER:	Oh, naturally.
GEORGIA LEE ENTERS.	ALIBI:	We'll find out. Here she comes now.
	GEORGIA:	Hello, you two.
	ELMER:	Hello, you beautiful creature.
SHE KISSES HIM	GEORGIA:	Why, Elmer, you sweet thing.
	ELMER:	Georgia Lee, I've been thinking it over.
	GEORGIA:	Well, tell me what you've decided.
	ELMER:	I like you.
	GEORGIA:	Well now that's funny, I like you too.
	ELMER:	You're wonderful.
	GEORGIA:	You're wonderful, too.
	ELMER:	And you're smart.
	GEORGIA:	You're smart too, Elmer.
	ELMER:	And you're SO beautiful.
	GEORGIA:	And you're SO..smart, Elmer.
		(SHE PATS HIM AND EXITS)

ed

ELMER: I should'a quit while I was ahead,
Terhune.

ALIBI: At least she thinks you're smart.

ELMER: Of course I am.

ALIBI: But you're always knocking people.

ELMER: Who have I knocked lately?

ALIBI: If it isn't Crash it's Bob Oates, or
Buddy, or Ralph Ward. I think I'd better give you
the loyalty test, Elmer.

ELMER: What's that?

ALIBI: Just a few questions I want to ask you.
First, some practice questions. What's the
opposite of sorrow?

ELMER: Joy.

ALIBI: Pleasure?

ELMER: Pain.

ALIBI: Woe?

ELMER: Giddap.

ALIBI: That'll do. Now, watch this one;
where's Washington?

ELMER: He's dead.

ALIBI: No, I mean the capitol of the United
States?

ELMER: Oh, we gave it all to Europe.

ALIBI: Elmer, do you promise to support the
Constitution?

ELMER: The what?

ALIBI: Constitution.

ed

	ELMER:	How can I? It's all I can do to support you.
	ALIBI:	I mean will you promise to be a loyal American?
	ELMER:	Oh, first, last and always.
SLAPS A MILITARY CAP ON HIM.	ALIBI:	That's all I wanted to know.
	ELMER:	What happened?
	ALIBI:	You're in the Army.
DISSOLVE TO:	ELMER:	I've been grafted!

(APPLAUSE)

ed

CORRIGAN AND   MUSIC: (RAY BROOME DOES A RUN ON THE FIDDLE)
THE BROOME BOYS.
                      CORRIGAN: That's a nice number, Ray. What is it?

                      RAY BROOME: I was just tunin' my fiddle.

                      CORRIGAN: Oh. Well, willya do me a favor?

                      RAY BROOME: Sure, Crash.

                      CORRIGAN: A few weeks ago...here on our ranch

                      you did a number. The folks said they'd like to

                      hear it again. How about it?

                      LEE BROOME: Sure it wasn't me who did it?

                      CORRIGAN: No, it was Ray...and of course I

                      helped out...here and there.

                      RAY BROOME: Oh, you mean, "Pop! Goes the Weasel."

                      CORRIGAN: That's what I mean, Pop. Go with the

                      weasel again, huh?

                      RAY BROOME: Sure!

                      MUSIC: ("POP GOES THE WEASEL")

DISSOLVE TO: (APPLAUSE)

ed

BOB OATES AND
GEORGIA LEE.

BOB OATES: I hope you're satisfied now that you've done OUR duet with Ralph Ward.

GEORGIA: Well, you and Crash were fighting like a couple of....

BOB OATES: Couple of what?

GEORGIA: Dopes.

BOB OATES: That's a fine way to talk.

GEORGIA: I'm sorry, Bob.

BOB OATES: After all I've done for you. Why, you're the first one I think about when I get up in the morning.

GEORGIA: That's funny, Crash says the same thing.

BOB OATES: Ah, Crash! I get up before he does! **Georgie**, is it because Crash has money and I'm just a horse wrangler? Is that's what's wrong?

GEORGIA: Don't be silly.

BOB OATES: You wouldn't marry a man for his money, would you?

GEORGIA: Of course not. All I want the man I marry, to have is a good disposition.

BOB OATES: Sure.

GEORGIA: Of course, if he DIDN'T **have** money he might be grouchy.

BOB OATES: I get it. Women are all alike.

GEORGIA: Don't be so cynical, Bob. Come on, let's sing our duet.

BOB OATES: No, Sir. I'll take Nellie.

GEORGIA: All RIGHT! Go ahead.

MUSIC: ("MY FILLY NELLIE"...BOB OATES)

GEORGIA: Bob.

BOB OATES: Huh?

GEORGIA: I'm sorry we argued. (SHE KISSES
             HIM ON THE FOREHEAD)

BOB OATES: To heck with Nellie!

DISSOLVE TO: MUSIC: (BUDDY IS DOODLING ON THE GUITAR)

BUDDY AND CRASH ON   CORRIGAN: What's the matter, Buddy?
THE BALE OF HAY
                            BUDDY: I'm sleepy.

                            CORRIGAN: Whatcha gonna do about it.

                            BUDDY: Play myself a lullaby.

                            CORRIGAN: Good idea. Here, I'll set the

             alarm so you can wake up for the applause.

                            MUSIC: ("SLEEP")

                            SOUND: ALARM CLOCK RINGS

ALIBI ENTERS.   BUDDY: (JUMPS UP)

L

ALIBI ENTERS.

ALIBI: Buddy, shame on you for sleepin'
Why don't you go to work?

BUDDY: Why should I work?

ALIBI: To make money.

BUDDY: What for?

ALIBI: So you wont have to work.

BUDDY: I don't have to work now.

ALIBI: Yeah. But where are ya?

BUDDY: Right here.

ALIBI: Can you prove it?

BUDDY: Sure.

ALIBI: Wanta make a bet?

BUDDY: Sure.

ALIBI: I'll bet you ten dollars you're
not here.

BUDDY: You'll bet me ten dollars I'm
not here?

ALIBI: That's what I said.

BUDDY: Oh, boy. And it's legal too.

ALIBI: Put your money in my hand.

BUDDY: No, you put your money in MY hand.

ALIBI: Okay. Now, you're not in
Pocatello are you?

BUDDY: Where's that?

ALIBI: Idaho.

BUDDY: Nope. I'm not there.

ALIBI: And you're not in Denver,
Colorado?

BUDDY: I've got a cousin there.

L

CRASH CORRIGAN'S RANCH
8-19-50

ALIBI: Who hasn't? So, if you're not
in Pocatello, and you're not in Denver, you
must be someplace else.

BUDDY: Sure, I'm here.

ALIBI: Look, if you're someplace else
how can you be here?

BUDDY: Oh, I can do it.

ALIBI TAKES THE MONEY.

ALIBI: Sorry, Buddy, I win.

BUDDY: I've been swindled.

ALIBI: Tell you what you do, Buddy.
Here comes Crash. Bet him TWENTY dollars.
You can't lose.

ALIBI EXITS...CRASH
        ENTERS.

BUDDY: Oh, Mr. Crash.

CORRIGAN: Hello, Buddy.

BUDDY: I'll bet you twenty dollars
you're not here.

CORRIGAN: No, Buddy. I don't want to take
your money.

BUDDY: Oh, but I'm gonna take YOUR
money.

CORRIGAN: In that case, I'll bet you.

BUDDY: Put your money in my hand.

CORRIGAN: I'd better hold it.

BUDDY: Okay. Now, you're not in
Pocatello.

CORRIGAN: Oh, no. I'm not in Pocatello.

BUDDY: And you're not in Denver, where
my cousin is?

CORRIGAN: Absolutely not. And thanks a

CORRIGAN STARTS TO
        EXIT.

lot. It's a pleasure to do business with
you, Buddy.

BUDDY:	Wait a minute!
CORRIGAN:	What's the matter?
BUDDY:	You forgot to give me my money.
CORRIGAN:	But I don't have your money.
BUDDY:	Sure, right there in your hand.
CORRIGAN:	Buddy, look. I'm not in Pocatello am I?
BUDDY:	No.
CORRIGAN:	And I'm not in Denver?
BUDDY:	No.
CORRIGAN:	So I MUST be someplace else.
BUDDY:	Yeah. So I win. Give me my money.
CORRIGAN:	Buddy, if I'm someplace else how can I POSSIBLY have your money. (HE EXITS)
BUDDY:	Help!

GEORGIA LEE ENTERS

GEORGIA:	What's the matter, Buddy?
BUDDY:	I made a couple of bad investments.
GEORGIA:	What happened?
BUDDY:	I was tooken.
GEORGIA:	You too?
BUDDY:	Aren't you here, either?
GEORGIA:	Listen, Buddy, to MY sad story.
MUSIC:	("I'VE BEEN TOOKEN"...GEORGIA LEE)

CUT TO: (APPLAUSE)

BOB OATES AND CORRIGAN   BOB OATES: No Sir! No more tradin' jobs
                                      with you or anybody.

L

CORRIGAN: It worked out okay.

BOB OATES: But next week Georgia Lee and
I sing our duet...AS usual.

TOE TO TOE AGAIN   CORRIGAN: Oh, yeah?

BOB OATES: Yeah.

CORRIGAN: Says who?

GEORGIA LEE POKES HER   GEORGIA: Says me.
HEAD BETWEEN THEM.
CORRIGAN: And that's an order. You have
fun, kids?

BOB & GEORGIA: Yeah. Did you?

CORRIGAN: Yeah. (TO AUDIENCE) Did you?

CAST: (CHEERS)

C.U. OF THE THREE   CORRIGAN: Then it's next week...same time
...on Corrigan's Ranch. 'Till then this is
Crash Corrigan saying, good night, thanks
everybody, and see you in church.

GROUP SHOT   THEME: (TO TIME)
(SUPER TITLES AND
CREDITS)

L

VIDEO	AUDIO
FILM SIG OPENING (1:30)	THEME: (RECORDED)
L.S. OR CRASH RIDING ALONG ROAD EN ROUTE TO MAIN GATE.	ANNCR: (O.S.) Here comes CRASH CORRIGAN ! ! Along the old Stage Coach Road where every hoof beats out action, adventure, secrets and surprises of the old West!
L.S. OUTSIDE MAIN GATE, CROWD SCENE, CRASH GALLOPS IN WAVING.	You're at CORRIGANVILLE, famous 2000-acre movie ranch where you can walk in the footsteps of the stars!...down the streets of Frontier Town, Cavalry Fort, and the Spanish Village. This is where movies come to life!
C.U. OF SIGN "CORRIGAN-VILLE"	Welcome to the old West's last frontier!
L.S. REVERSE SHOT OF CROWD.	And this is you...wide-eyed and beaming with anticipation as you follow Crash on your first tour of his great ranch, down main street...past Sam's Saloon, the Wells-Fargo office and the General Store. You're about to enjoy 90 minutes of real out-in-the-open cowboy fun!
L.S. MAIN STREET; CRASH APPROACHES HITCHING RACK, DISMOUNTS, TIES HORSE AND STRIDES TOWARD TRADING POST.	Your host is none other than that famous star of "The Range Busters" and "Buckskin Rangers"---the real-life dare-devil, the popular bronc busting, roping and gun-toting movie star, "Crash" Corrigan, himself. Hi,
END OF FILM CLIP CUT TO:	Crash! 6:01:30

VIDEO	AUDIO
BOB OATES ENTERS, HANGS SADDLE ON RACK AND RESPONDS.	BOB: Hi, there. I'm not Crash...I'm Bob Oates. I think Crash is over there some place. (POINTS L.)
PAN TO:	
POLLY AND MARY ELLEN	POLLY: Oh, heavens, I'm not Crash. I'm Polly. Mary Ellen, where's Crash?
CUT TO:	MARY: I think he's over there. (POINTS R.)
WALLY, HE STANDS C. AT END OF HITCHING RACK.	WALLY: Hi. I'm Wally Dempsey. Here comes Crash now. (WHEN CRASH CROSSES TO
CRASH ENTERS, CARRYING SADDLE, WALKS UP TO WALLY.	HIM LOOKING FOR PLACE TO PUT SADDLE) What kept ya?
	CRASH: (HANDS WALLY THE SADDLE) Take this.
WALLY STAGGERS OUT WITH SADDLE.	WALLY: (TAKES SADDLE, WEIGHT ALMOST KNOCKING HIM OVER. EXITS)
	CRASH: Welcome to the ranch, folks. Say, I've got a lot to say to you in just a minute. Meantime, see Buddy Kelley and the boys. They have a song for ya.
PAN TO:	
INSTRUMENTAL GROUP	SONG: _____ BUDDY AND BAND
CRASH, PATS BUDDY ON SHOULDER AND CROSSES CENTER	CRASH: Say, Buddy, that was fine. (CROSSES CENTER) Folks, we have a little rule here at Corriganville. That is: if you come as a stranger you must leave as a friend. So, just relax and have fun for the next 90 minutes. The gang has worked up a swell show for you and...a little later on... (CONT)

VIDEO   AUDIO

CRASH CONTINUES   (CONT) I have a wonderful western story
                              to tell you about.

BOB CROSSES TO CRASH   BOB: Hey, Crash! I know what let's do.

                              CRASH: What? Bob?

                              BOB: Tonight let's just talk about the
                              old West...you know, like cowboyin', hold-ups,
                              how you make your western pictures...stuff
                              like that.

                              CRASH: Isn't that what we always talk about?

                              BOB: Yeah...but somebody always comes
                              around to change the subject.

                              CRASH: Not tonight, Bob. This is Corriganvill
                              the old West's last frontier, the home oft
                              the "Range Busters"...and if we catch anybody
                              talking anything but western talk we'll.. .

                              BOB: Fine 'em a dollar.

WALLY ENTERS.   CRASH: Good idea.

                              WALLY: Top of the evening to you, fellas.

                              BOB: Top of the evening? Crash.

                              CRASH: Not very western do you think?

                              BOB: That'll cost you a dollar, Wally.

                              WALLY: A dollar? What for?

                              BOB: New rule.

                              CRASH: We're fining everybody a dollar every
                              time they so much as mention something that
                              isn't western.

WALLY GIVES BOB A DOLLAR.   BOB: Got anything else you want to talk
                              about?

                              WALLY: Well, I was gonna tell you about
                                      Custer's last stand.

VIDEO

<u>AUDIO</u>

CRASH: That's more like it...that's one of the classic stories of the old West. What were you gonna say about Custer's Last Stand.

WALLY: I got a chance to buy it.

BOB: Wait a minute...you have a chance to buy Custer's Last Stand...way up there in the Little Big Horn Mountains in Wyoming?

WALLY HANDS HIM SECOND DOLLAR.

WALLY: No...this is a hot dog stand down at the beach....I know, here's your dollar.

CRASH: Business is good today. What are you gonna play on that banjo?

WALLY HANDS HIM THIRD DOLLAR.

WALLY: Here's another dollar.

BOB: What is it?

WALLY: "Swanee River"....and I hope it's worth it.

CUT TO:

<u>BANJO SOLO: "SWANEE RIVER" WALLY DEMPSEY</u>

C.U. "SEARS ROEBUCK CATALOG"PULL BACK TO REVEAL POLLY AND MARY ELLEN LOOKING COVETOUSLY AT FASHIONS.

POLLY: Oh, Mary Ellen...look at all these city dresses in here. I wish I had a pretty dress.

MARY: Don't let Crash hear you talking like that.

POLLY: Why not?

MARY: He's fining everybody on the ranch a dollar every time they talk about anything that's dude.

VIDEO	AUDIO
	POLLY: Yeah...but it isn't human nature for a gal not to want nice things...especially western gals who don't get into town very often anyway....Don't you think....
	MARY: (INTERRUPTING) Shhhh! Here comes Crash now....(OBVIOUSLY FOR CRASH'S EARS) Yes, gal, that's a real saddle...look at
CRASH ENTERS AND STUDIES THEM.	them skirts...and that seat...you could ride fer miles and never....oh, hello, Crash.
	CRASH: Howdy, gals...say now if you two don't make a fella feel proud of his own ranch. To see two such pretty gals...just as western as you can be. Thinkin' of buyin' a new saddle?
	POLLY: Uh....yes, Crash...there's one here... brand new style. It would look awful nice
CRASH ANGLES BEHIND THEM TO GET A BETTER LOOK AT THE CATALOG.	on me....I mean, it looks comfortable to ride..
	CRASH: (HE'S WISE TO THEIR TRICKERY NOW) Yes, I see what you mean. First saddle I ever did see with a plunging neck line. It'll start a whole new trend out on the range.
	MARY: Plunging.neckline? Why, Polly! You XXXXXX lost our place in the catalog. Get back to the saddle section...we don't want to look at those horrible dude dresses.
	CRASH: All right, girls. That'll be a dollar from each of you. Right's right, ya know.
GIRLS GIVE HIM MONEY.	POLLY: Okay, then, let's go.
	CRASH: Where ya goin'?
	MARY: To get our dollar's worth.
DARLING SISTERS SING	SONG: "MR. SEARS AND ROEBUCK" starts

VIDEO

CUT TO:

BOB AND WALLY

AUDIO

WALLY: Hey, Bob, doesn't the Constitution say we get free speech in America?

BOB: Yep...that's what it says.

WALLY: How much does it cost?

BOB: Wally, it doesn't cost a nickel. That's why it's called "free speech".

WALLY: Then where does Crash get off waylayin me for a dollar everytime I open my yap?

BOB: Oh, it isn't that bad, Wally!

WALLY: Oh, no? I open my mouth and HE says "dollar". (OPENS AND SHUTS HIS MOUTH THREE TIMES) Dollar, dollar, dollar. That's better'n strikin' oil.

BOB: Crash is just trying to teach you all a lesson. You see, this is Corriganville, the old West's last frontier. He wants us to live it...and talk it...so that we can tell the folks from the city how it REALLY was in the old days. That's all. He's teaching a lesso

WALLY: I know what lesson, too..."Silence is golden"...but he's foolin' with dynamite w en he fools with me. I'll get my money back.

BOB: How?

WALLY: I'll do it. Crash isn't the only one who knows all these fancy tricks. I got a thing or two up my sleeve.

BOB: Let me see. (HE LOOKS UP WALLY'S SLEEVE) Hey, guess what.

VIDEO	AUDIO
	WALLY: What's the matter?
	BOB: It's dark up here.
LIGHTS: SPECIAL NIGHT EFFECT.	MUSIC: SNEAK IN AN INTRO...SOFTLY
	WALLY: Dark out here, too.
	BOB: (PEERING INTENTLY INTO SPACE) Herd's gettin' a little spooky, too.
	WALLY: What herd?
	BOB: Out there.
	WALLY: Oh.
	BOB: Guess I'd better sing to 'em...'fore they stampede.
	WALLY: Yeah...that'd be bad....I guess.
DISSOLVE TO:	SONG: "SILVER ON THE SAGE" BOB OATES
POLLY AND CRASH	CRASH: Gosh, wasn't that a perty song, Miss Polly?
	POLLY: I'm afraid to talk...it'd cost me a dollar already.
	CRASH: Aw, Miss Polly...I wouldn't keep your money. Say what you think.
	POLLY: It was an awfully pretty song.
	CRASH: Oh, now, it wasn't THAT pretty was it?
	POLLY: Yes it was. What did Bob Oates mean when he said that he was going to sing to keep the herd from stampeding?
	CRASH: That's true, Miss Polly.
	(GO INTO DISCUSSION OF STAMPEDES) WHAT MAKES A HERD STAMPEDE? WHY DOES MUSIC QUIET THEM? HAVE YOU EVER BEEN IN A STAMPEDE? HOW DO YOU STOP A STAMPEDE? HAS THERE EVER BEEN A STAMPEDE AT CORRIGAN'S MOVIE RANCH? ETC.

VIDEO   AUDIO

                                         (CONT) (STAMPEDES)
                                              TELL US AN UNSUAL STORY ABOUT A
                                              STAMPEDE (SHORT)

WALLY ENTERS, STEALTHILY   WALLY: Okay, XXXXX reach!
HE CREEPS UP ON CRASH.
                                  CRASH: Wally! What's the matter with you?

                                  WALLY: Take my money willya? Well, you

                                  met your match this time, you Range Buster.

                                  BIZ: CRASH SUDDENLY DISARMS WALLY. WALLY
                                            EXPLAINS THAT HE WAS ONLY TRYING TO
                                            GET HIS MONEY BACK. CRASH TELLS HIM
                                            THAT THERE ARE A FEW THINGS HE SHOULD
                                            BE SURE OF BEFORE HE TRIES TO USE
                                            A GUN INSTEAD OF HIS HEAD.
                                            BOB ENTERS AND ASKS CRASH TO SHOW US
                                            ALL WHAT TO DO IN CASE WE SHOULD EVER
                                            BE THE VICTIMS OF A HOLDUP. WALLY,
                                            OF COURSE, HAS HIS OWN IDEAS. BUT
                                            CRASH DEMONSTRATES...FIRST, BY
                                            LETTING WALLY GIVE HIS VERSION AND,
                                            THEN, BY SHOWING WHAT A RANGE BUSTERS
                                            DOES.

VIDEO	AUDIO
	CRASH: (SUMMARIZING) But, you want to remember, of course, that you can always get more money. .but you can never get another life. Remember the man who said, "He who steals my purse steals trash". The best thing you can do if somebody pulls a gun on you is to do what he says...only stay alert... so that when the law asks you to identify the scoundrel you'll be able to do it.
	CUE:FOR SONG: Remember, life is precious
CUT TO:	and is not to be wasted.
BOB AND MARY ELLEN.	SONG: "I'D RATHER SPEND MY LIFE WITH YOU"
CUT TO:	
CRASH, ALONE	CRASH: Say, that was a nice song, wasn't it? That's just how I feel about making western pictures. In a manner of speaking I'm spending /XXXXXXXXX my life with you westerners... folks like myself. You invite me into your home every Saturday night. So to return the favor I'm going to invite you out to my ranch every Sunday. You stay tuned to our show and I'll tell you more about that later. (CALLS) Oh, Polly! Mary Ellen! Wally! Bob! Come here.
THEY ALL ENTER AND GATHER AROUND CRASH.	ALL: What do you want, Crash? Etc. Etc.
	CRASH: How much did I fine all you people for not talking western talk earlier in the show?
	CAST: AD LIB

HE HANDS THEM SILVER
DOLLARS.

CRASH: Okay, here's your money back. Here's your XXXXX dollar Mary Ellen. Polly, this is yours. Well, I guess that does it.

WALLY: How about mine...three dollars I've got coming.

CRASH: Bob has two of them.

BOB GIVES WALLY TWO
DOLLAR BILLS.

BOB: Here you are, Wally.

WALLY: What about the other one?

CRASH HOLDS A SILVER
DOLLAR IN HIS FINGERS.

CRASH: You mean this one?

WALLY: Yeah, that one.

CRASH: Well, now, this particular dollar reminds me of a story.

WALLY: I know the story. It's about how I lost three dollars.

BOB: No, Wally, that's not the story Crash has in mind at all.

CRASH: The story I have in mind is called "THE SILVER TRAIL". The hero of the story is a friend of mine...Rex Lease. But before I tell you this story there's something I want you all to remember. As soon as this story is over...about an hour from now...we'll all meet right back here in front of the General Store for something important.

BOB: Okay, Crash, let's have the story.

CRASH: Well, one day...(AD LIB INTO FILM)

MOOD MUSIC: B.G.

FILM

CUE IN PAST MAIN TITLE TO
FIRST SCENE...START LAP
DISSOLVE OF FILM WHEN
CRASH CLASPS HIS HANDS
TOGETHER.

CRASH: (CONTINUE AD LIB INTRO)

FILM: "THE SILVER TRAIL"   CLEAR

VIDEO	AUDIO

FILM BREAK-IN BY CRASH

(APPROX. 15 min. IN
EXT. SCENE, REX LEASE
LEAVES, CRASH WALKS IN, L.

CRASH: Well, I'm not going to follow
Rex Lease. He's headed for trouble. Not
that I wouldn't like to join the excitement
on "The Silver Trail" but my first duty
right now is to you...and I'm interested
in keeping you from having trouble to. So

(PULLS GUN AND POINTS
OFF SCENE)

Maybe you'd better listen to this......

******INSERT COMMERCIAL OR PUBLIC SERVICE SPOT******

CRASH: Okay, let's get back on that "Silver
Trail" with Rex Lease. And, don't fogget, when
we get to the end of that trail I have somethin
very important to tell you.

ROLL THE FILM   "SILVER TRAIL"   TO CONCLUSION

AT END OF FILM:

KILL THE MAIN TITLE
VIDEO FADE ON LAST SCENE TO:

LV   HOLD MUSICAL CURTAIN FROM FILM SOUND TO BUTTON

CRASH MATCHES OR REACTS
TO ACTION AT FINAL SCENE.
PULL BACK TO REVEAL THE
CAST DOING LIKEWISE.

CRASH: Well, there goes Rex Lease down
"The Silver Trail". Swell story, wasn't it?
BOB: You bet. What's the story for next
week, Crash?
CRASH: Tell you in a minute. First, here's
that news I promised the folks: Neighbors,

(INTO INVITATION TO VISIT THE RANCH
 SEE MOVIE SETS,
 MOVIES IN THE MAKING,
 BRING PICNIC LUNCH,
 RIDE HORSES, ETC.
 NOMINAL CHARGE OF 60 and 30 cents.

VIDEO	AUDIO	
	BOB:	Crash, how do you get to Corriganville from...say...Pasadena.
CUT TO:		
CU OF MAP.	CRASH:	Well, whether you live in Pasadena, East Los Angeles, Long Beach, Santa Monica or Los Angeles proper...all roads lead to Corriganville. Just go out Ventura Boulevard to Topango Canyon Boulevard...turn right and drive to the town of "Chatworth". Now you're on Highway 118. Follow it over historic Santa Susanna Pass for a few miles...you'll see signs leading to the ranch all along your way. But, now you come to a big sign that says, "CORRIGANVILLE". Soon after that you'll see the turn-off that leads you right to my main gate. Don't forget...tomorrow...Sunday, is visitor day at the only movie ranch of its kind in the world. Come on out and help us have some of that fun.
WALLY ENTERS BREATHLESSLY.	WALLY:	XXXXX Hey, Crash'. You got a telegram'.
CRASH TAKES TELEGRAM.	CRASH:	Thanks, Wally. (HE OPENS IT, READS) Hey! This is BIG news!
	POLLY:	What does it say, Crash?
	BOB:	Yeah, don't keep us in suspense'
	CRASH:	Sorry, I wont be able to tell you until next week...right now, it's hymn time on the ranch.

VIDEO   AUDIO

DISSOLVE TO:

BOB AND CAST, WHO SING.   HYMN: "   "

                                    AFTER ONE CHORUS CONTINUE HUMMINNG FOR

CRASH, CROSSES DOWN CENTER   CRASH: (OVER MUSIC) Well, you came as a
                               friend. I hope and pray you're leaving as a
                               stranger. To all of you...sleep well, keep
                               happy and drive carefully. And speakin' of
                               driving we'd all be happy to have you drive
                               out to the ranch tomorrow. If you can't make
                               it then...be sure to meet us here on Channel
                               Eleven...KTTV....at Six oclock next Saturday
                               evening. We'll have another big show...a
                               great big surprise, and an exciting western
                               adventure, "   " starring
PAN TO CAST   _____. So, for Bob, Polly, Wally,
C.U. OF CORRIGAN   Mary Ellen, Buddy Kelley and the Corriganville
                               this is your friend, Crash Corrigan, saying:
                                                           may you
                               goodbye, God bless you, and/ride the trail
DISSOLVE TO: health and happiness until we meet again.

DRUM: (1:20)

CU OF SIGN OVER GATE:
"CORRIGANVILLE"   ANNCR: Yes, it's so long for now to
                                Corriganville, the world's most exciting
                                ranch...and it's owner, Crash Corrigan'!

ROLL DRUM

"WRITTEN BY BOB OLSEN"
TECH. DIR. --BOB ELLIS"
DIR. BY BOB HIESTAND
"THE CRASH CORRIGAN SHOW
        with
BOB OATES
THE DARLING SISTERS
WALLY DEMPSEY
     and starring

RAY "CRASH" CORRIGAN.

DISSOLVE TO:

VIDEO   AUDIO

FILM:

CU SIGN: CORRIGANVILLE
CAMERA PANS DOWN AND
DOLLIES BACK, DISCLOSING
CRASH AT GATE WAVING   ANNCR: Remember, you have a date next week
GOODBYE TO US.
                                         for "The Crash Corrigan Show"..

                                         same time...same place...for more

                                         action, adventure, secrets and

                                         surprises of the old West's last

                                         frontier...Crash Corrigan's Movie

                                         Ranch'. So long.....

FADE OUT   MUSIC: TO TIME

Do you have the most comprehensive reference book ever written on the Ray "Crash" Corrigan Movie Ranch aka Corriganville? Now is your chance to purchase your own copy of this immense book.

The Definitive True History of the Ray "Crash" Corrigan Movie Ranch

by Jerry L. Schneider